DOG

TURTLE

ELEPHANT

DEER

SQUIRREL

FROG

TIGER

DUCK

CAT

RABBIT

BEAR

YAK

LEMUR

FERRET

MEERKAT

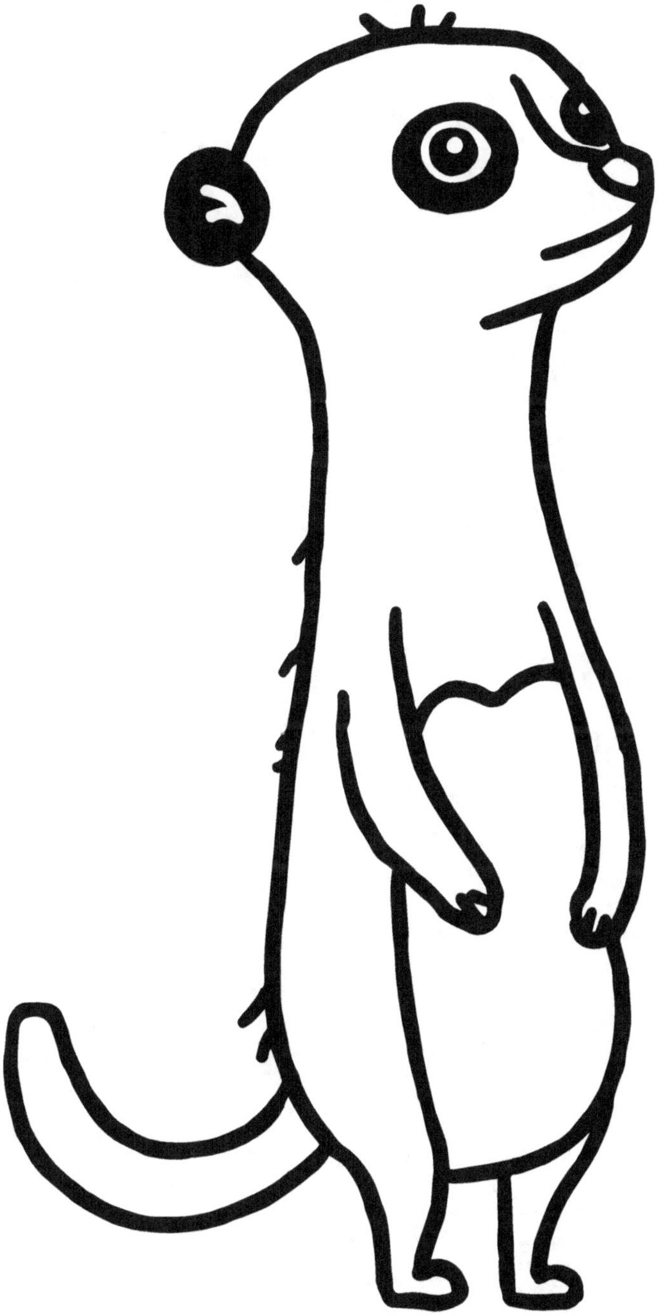

SNAKE

BEAR

PIG

FOX

OWL

HEDGEHOG

MOUSE

TIGER

SHARK

PENGUIN

www.ingramcontent.com/pod-product-compliance
Lightning Source LLC
Chambersburg PA
CBHW062234220526
45471CB00009B/3472
* 9 7 9 8 3 2 0 4 0 3 3 8 0 *